How to Make Cornhusk Dolls

Man and lady with churn.

HOW TO MAKE
Cornhusk Dolls

By Ruth Wendorff

arco
New York

To Louise Yukl

Photographs by Franz Wendorff

Published by Arco Publishing Company, Inc.
219 Park Avenue South, New York, N.Y. 10003

Library of Congress Catalog Card Number 72-90906

ISBN 0-668-02883-1

Printed in the United States of America

Acknowledgement is made to the following for cooperation and assistance in the preparation of this book:*Christian Science Monitor,* Boston, Massachusetts; *World Book Encyclopedia,* Chicago, Illinois; Garden Center of Greater Cleveland; Colony Garden Club, Cleveland Heights, Ohio; Garden Club of the Hills, Euclid, Ohio; Master's United Methodist Church, Euclid, Ohio.

Contents

How to Make Cornhusk Dolls

1

Introducing Cornhusk Dolls and Beverly Banci

Remember when everybody did something with his hands—whittling, tatting, embroidering, crocheting, or knitting? That was a long time ago. Now, we're swinging back to arts and crafts as hobbies as well as vocations. Using our talents to create something beautiful or useful brings joy and satisfaction.

Dolls can be made from almost anything. Scraps of cloth, old stockings, and pieces of felt or leather are excellent materials for doll-making. Corncobs and cornhusks work up well and so do peanuts and acorns. A clever person can make a doll from a spool or clothespin. Many doll-makers like a challenge and use paper, cardboard, hairpins, wire, raffia, string, and rubber from old inner-tubes.

In the early days of history, natives of the plains wrapped grasses, straw or cornhusks into doll shapes. Forest dwellers used wood, bark and roots. Those who lived near the sea used shells and seaweed. In hot countries, palm leaves are still woven into dolls. Many Mexican dolls are made of rags, wood or clay. Others are braided of leaf fibers. Very sturdy dolls are made of straw, cornhusks and pieces of cornstalk. These are painted in brilliant colors.

Cornhusks can be crocheted or woven into mats, but dolls are much more fun to make. With a little practice most people become adept enough to make a doll. From a handful of cornhusks to a

11

Pilgrim family.

finished doll—would you guess two hours? One hour? Wrong, both times. A delightful doll can be made in only 20 or 30 minutes!

This book shows how to make cornhusk dolls and accessories the Banci way. Doll-making can become a fascinating hobby or just a satisfying way to make decorations for your home.

There are several different procedures to follow in making the various cornhusk dolls. Simple lapel-ornaments can be put together in a few minutes. Extremely complicated Christmas tree-ornament dolls with layers and layers of petticoats and skirts take considerably longer.

Favorite cornhusk dolls are pilgrims with traditional costumes. Dresses, aprons and caps clothe the women and girls. Men and boys wear knickers and carry muskets made from weed stalks.

Besides the obvious Thanksgiving-pilgrim table decorations, many other kinds of display are possible. A collection of dolls shown in a glass case becomes an ever-growing family whenever the collector makes a lucky find. Where do you buy these dolls? In hobby shops, florist shops, Historical Society museums, and at art shows, doll fairs, and bazaars. Many cornhusk dolls are imported. Some have wooden heads; others have apple heads. Most of them are made entirely from cornhusks.

Indian children used to play with dolls made of corncobs, cornsilk hair and husk clothing. Today's cornhusk dolls are not meant to be played with; their function is almost entirely decorative. Although the traditional Thanksgiving pilgrim family is the most popular, other kinds of dolls rank close behind them. These are the nationality dolls from Czechoslovakia and Mexico. Dolls from our own Appalachian mountains are favorites with many.

As table settings at Thanksgiving time, the cornhusk dolls present an interesting and personal decoration. When family members gather for dinner and see a doll at each place, they will appreciate and remember them for a long time. It is a nice gesture to give the dolls as souvenirs of special dinners and celebrations. You can be assured that they will be carried home and treasured for years. Cornhusk dolls will keep indefinitely, if cared for properly and packed carefully.

Wall plaques made of weathered boards with shelves of fungi holding dolls become very effective conversation pieces, especially with an Early American decor. Another striking use of this medium is in a crucifixion plaque using a background of burlap or velvet, with the figure on the cross made of cornhusks. The cross itself can be made of either twigs or pieces of husk.

Unusual effects can be made with flower arrangements. Have your doll busily watering the flowers or plants with a tiny sprinkling can. Live flowers may be augmented with artificial flowers made from the versatile husks.

A birthday party gives you an ideal chance to plan and make a surprise centerpiece. Important events in the life of the birthday boy or girl can be portrayed by cornhusk people arranged on a tray with plants, flowers, furniture and animals. A circus centerpiece can include animals and clowns. If you allow your imagination to run, you'll be amazed at the number of decorative ideas that will come to

Girl with sprinkling can.

you. Each doll is different with no set rules for its manufacture. You follow your own inclinations. This is one of the joys of cornhusk doll-making: the absolute freedom to make your own creations.

Beverly Banci's interest in cornhusk dolls began with a visit to a hobby show and fair organized by the Historical Society of Burton,

Beverly with students.

Ohio. After being trained at Cleveland's John Huntington Art Institute, Beverly taught arts and crafts in library classes in Euclid, Ohio. Now considered an expert, after making dolls for ten years, Mrs. Banci demonstrates her art at club meetings and doll fairs. She makes at least a dozen dolls ahead of time, so there will be plenty ready to display. As soon she sits down to start working with the husks, a crowd gathers, watches and listens. She demonstrates and lectures continuously for three hours at the doll fairs. Every doll that she makes is usually sold while still wet!

The Banci family spend much of their vacation time out-of-doors, traveling and camping. They are always on the lookout for weeds and other natural products with which to make home decorations. The family Christmas tree each year is made from this-tles which are dyed a dark green, then decorated with tiny poinsettia lights and bead garlands. Cornhusk dolls circle the tree.

The whole family cooperates to further each member's creative ability. Laura and Loretta, both art students, often help their mother with her projects. One of these is the Art Barn, a school for arts and crafts that Beverly set up in their barn-red garage. Another is her frequent silhouette-cutting jobs for local fund-raising events.

Mrs. Banci is very active in the Willowick Art Club, helping with its art shows as well as showing her work in watercolor, oil, and painting on burlap with gouache. Besides her lectures and demonstrations of cornhusk doll-making, Mrs. Banci makes dolls to order. She recently had a very interesting task: making a man doll doing carpentry. He had to match a Czechoslovakian lady doll sewing a cross-stitch sampler.

Mrs. Banci's cornhusk dolls have also turned into a money-mak-ing project which spreads her knowledge and talent throughout her community. Teaching basic skills and helping find and develop the hidden talents of her students have combined to enrich Beverly Banci's life.

In this book, we hope that you will find help and inspiration from the instructions and pictures of Mrs. Banci's dolls.

2

Materials, Equipment, Preparation and Storage

MATERIALS

For Mrs. Banci, the most difficult part of making cornhusk dolls is finding the proper materials. She always uses husks from field corn. It's possible to make dolls from sweet cornhusks, but those husks are so fragile and small that work with them is often wasted. They tend to curl up tightly when dry, and don't hold up well under handling. Besides, it's fun to take a ride out into the country to look for field corn.

If you live in the corn belt, you'll be able to find field corn. Watch for tall corn, since field corn grows much taller than sweet corn. When you see some, approach the farmer, explain what you want, and ask to buy a bushel of corn. He'll probably be glad to sell you some. He might even **give** you the husks if you give back the corn. The next year, take the farmer's wife a doll. She'll make sure that you have enough cornhusks for the rest of your life.

Most corn is now picked by machine, so getting the husks can be a difficult process. Timing is important. You must wait until the corn is fully matured, but you have to get there before the machinery does. When the harvesters go into the fields and start picking, the machinery strips everything and grinds up what isn't used. Corn pickers harvest the ripe ears of corn; field choppers chop

17

the whole plants (ears, stalks, leaves) into silage for feed.

If you don't live in corn country or prefer to buy the husk in town, try the hobby shops, florist shops, grocery stores, country stores and fairs. Indian corn often produces colored husks of pink, red, maroon or brown. These can be bought at fairs, apple festivals, and stores handling decorations for Halloween and Thanksgiving. Buy 1 or 2 complete stalks. All parts of the plant are useful.

Besides cornhusks, try working with some leaves. They're brittle and not as easily worked, but they have a lovely green color and can be used for the long straight pieces in capes, furniture and rugs. Save the cornsilk for hair and beards. Even the tassel can be used as a tiny tree!

Materials for decorating the dolls range from tiny berries and seeds to artificial flowers, ribbons, and decorative candies such as you use on cupcakes and cookies.

The proper storage of your supplies will save you time as well as space. A tackle box will keep materials separate from each other and facilitate doll-making. If you prefer something larger and lighter, a suitcase with small boxes inside works admirably. Mrs. Banci uses an overnight case with the cosmetic tray functioning as the organizer of clips, rubber bands, wire, etc.

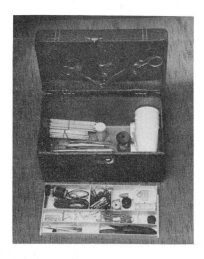

Overnight case with equipment.

EQUIPMENT

In addition to husks, you will need some very simple equipment. The list looks rather long, but most of the materials will be found around the house.

A squeeze bottle of household glue
Flexible wire
Drinking straws
Bobby pins
Short pieces of wood or bark
Vegetable dyes
Small pieces of dress materials
Straight pins
Heavy-duty shears
Hair clips
Styrofoam cups
Rubber bands
Felt-tipped pens
Tissues
Curved scissors

A tray to hold everything while you work will save much clean-up time by keeping the husk snippings and drops of water off the table or floor.

A large pitcher or pan of water for dipping the husks is necessary. Keep a spray bottle of water handy, too. The husks must be kept moist while you work them because they become brittle and unmanageable when dry.

There are different ways of keeping the wet husks motionless until they dry. You may pin some parts; others need a clamp. It depends on the thickness and shape of the part of the doll on which you are working. The parts which are too round and puffy to be clamped can be held with a rubber band. Many can be tied successfully with a strip of husk. After the doll is dry, cut off the tying strips.

Two pairs of scissors are all you need for cutting. The heavy-duty shears are used to cut the husk from the cob and also to cut through the wires. A smaller, more delicate pair of scissors, curved if you have them, will trim husks, hair and whiskers neatly. Dry your scissors carefully each time you put them away. A quick swipe with an oily cloth will ensure rust-free scissors.

PREPARATION

Immediately after you get your husks, spread them out to dry. Lay them onto sheets of newspaper on the floor of the garage, porch or a room with good ventilation. It will take several days for them to dry thoroughly. Never leave them on the ground because worms may burrow up into them, thus ruining the husks. Mildew will also spoil the husks. When completely dry, keep them in a dry place.

The husks may be dyed in order to add color to your dolls and arrangements. Make dye from food coloring or vegetable dyes such as those used to color Easter eggs. Follow directions on the package. Tiny bottles of the liquid dye used to color cake frostings offer an easy way to measure the drops. Soak the husks in your dye solution for from 15 to 30 minutes, depending on the shade of the color you want. Spread the dyed husks out on pads of newspaper and allow to dry thoroughly before you store them away.

Threads may be woven through the husks used for skirts, to give the impression of stripes. These may even be painted on with pen and ink or felt-tipped pens. This treatment is especially effective when making a group of dolls of different nationalities. The different modes of costume can be quickly and easily reproduced by just adding the distinctive patterns of the different countries your dolls represent. Many people like to dress their dolls in percale and gingham, using the solid colors in partnership with tiny prints. A straight piece of material gathered at the waist and tied on with a ribbon makes a beautiful skirt. Don't glue the skirt to the waist of the doll. When you're ready to store the dolls, just untie the ribbon, remove the skirt, and pack them both flat. When you're ready to display the dolls again, you may put the skirt back on or try some other fabric or color.

Beverly and the author put finishing touches on a clown and a lady.

STORAGE

Spray your storage boxes with insect killer. Don't spray the husks themselves, because there is oil in the spray which might discolor them. Spraying the boxes will kill all insects that might attack the husks.

When working with bark to set the dolls upon, dry the bark in the oven before using it. This procedure removes all moisture and prevents warping. Drying in the oven also kills all insect life in the bark.

When ready to store your dolls in the sprayed box, lay the dolls in carefully, separating them from each other with crumpled tissue paper. Store the box in a dry place such as an attic or linen closet.

Now that you have all your materials and equipment, it's time to begin to make a doll.

3

The All-in-One Lady Doll

The husks from one ear of corn will make one doll. Break off the corncob and discard it. Dip the whole husk into water and soak for a few seconds. Then take it out of the water, let drip, and cut off the stem end with scissors. Keep this bottom piece. It makes a perfect poppy for future decorations using flowers.

Pick out your very best pieces of different sizes of husk, as

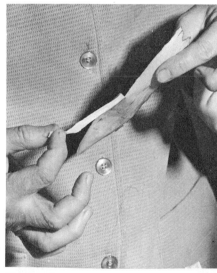

Dip whole husk in water and allow it to drip.

Tear tying strips from a large husk.

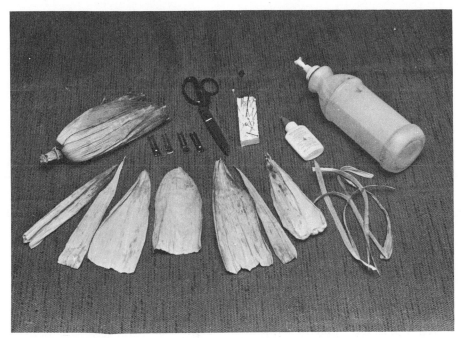

Equipment and materials needed for the lady doll.

follows: longest pieces for the front and back of dress, medium size piece for the apron, 2 small pieces for the sleeves, and 2 slightly smaller for the arms.

Tear tying strips from a long husk and keep them handy in a little pile. A tip on tying with the strips: experiment with them. When pulling on the strips, you'll break several until you find just the right tension to use. Practice. Cornhusks vary in texture and strength. Dip them in water often while you're working with your dolls.

Spread out the wet husks in this order: apron in the middle, then on each side, an arm piece, a sleeve piece, a skirt piece.

Hold arm and sleeve pieces facing each other; put the apron piece in the middle. Now place the skirt pieces on opposite sides of the apron. Gather them all together and squeeze tightly. Tie securely 2" from the top.

Roll this 2" length into a ball and pad it with husk or paper, wrapping around and around until the head is the size you want.

Flip over the arm pieces, then the dress pieces, then the apron,

Hold pieces of husk like this.

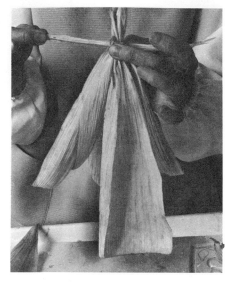

Tie tightly 2" from the end.

Pad and wrap head.

Flip over husks one at a time.

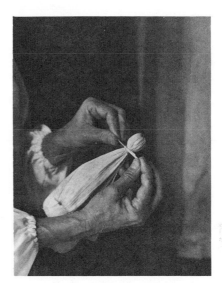

Smooth each one over the head.   Tie around neck.

smoothing each one in turn over this top ball. Pay special attention to the face area. The apron piece should be the finest husk that you have, so the face will be smooth and pretty.

Squeeze all the husks together tightly. Tie a strip around the neck and pull it as hard as you can without breaking it. The husks must be wet and pliable, so spray or dip them occasionally in water.

Pull and shape the skirt pieces into place and pin the side seams. Make a roll of husk or paper for padding and insert it into the chest cavity. Leave the arm and sleeve husks sticking out straight while you tie another strip around the waist. Tie it at the back and leave the ends long. They will become apron strings when the doll is finished.

Hold a wire against the doll to measure the correct length from fingertip to fingertip. It should be about 7 inches long. Cut with heavy-duty shears.

Insert this wire through the neck, keeping it under the arm and sleeve husks. Wrap arm piece around wire, then the sleeve piece around the arm, pinning as you go. Puff the sleeve up nicely. Tie a strip at the wrist, about ½" from the end of the arm. Trim off any

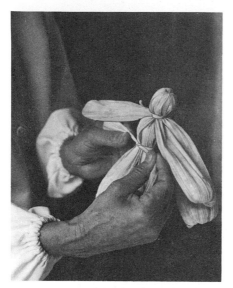

Tie at waist.

Insert wire.

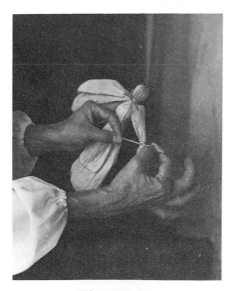

Tie at wrist.

Cut off husk at end of hand.

Insert cup.

Making the lady's hat.

extra uneven pieces to make the hand natural-looking. Form the other arm in the same way.

Your doll's head and arms are now done, and you're almost finished. Squeeze some glue up under the skirt near the waistline. Push in more stuffing to make the lady's hips. Insert a styrofoam cup. Clamp or pin it securely all around the bottom.

Trim the apron. Bend the arms into any shape you wish them to take. If you want the hands to hold the apron, bend them down now while the doll is still wet. Pin each hand to a corner of the apron.

For the lady's bonnet, cut a rectangular piece of husk 3" x 5". Fold back ¼" along the shorter edge and lay it across the head from side to side, holding it down snugly against the head. Fold the sides of the bonnet toward the back of the head; then pull the rest of the husk straight down across the back. You may alter the style by pulling the back of the bonnet down first, and **then** folding the sides back. (Here's where you can have fun designing different hat styles.) Pin hat firmly to head.

Allow your doll to dry. This may take several hours, or overnight, depending on how wet your husks were. As you continue to make the dolls, you'll find out just how wet the husks must be. Many people like to put their dolls in the gas oven with only the pilot light on. This is a perfect place to dry them, because they're out of the way and can't be knocked over. An open fireplace is another good drying place, doing the job much more quickly, but be careful that your doll isn't too close to the fire. If you don't have a gas oven or a fireplace, dry them on a shelf in any room that has good ventilation.

As soon as the doll is perfectly dry, remove the pins from the skirt. Run a line of glue around the outside of the styrofoam cup. Insert cup into doll. Apply a thin line of household glue to side seam of skirt; clamp with either hair clips, bobby pins, or paper clips. At this time, arrange some curls under the hat, allowing them to fall around the face in a pleasing coiffure. Curls may be made of husk, cornsilk, yarn, crepe paper, burlap ravelings, cotton, thread or real hair. (See Chapter 6 for different kinds of hair.) Glue hair to hat, and hat to head.

Smear the top side of the the apron with glue. Then fill it with any of a variety of things, such as bittersweet berries, rose hips, flower seeds, oats, wheat, straw flowers or decorating candies. Allow the glue to set completely, usually only an hour.

After the glue has dried, carefully remove all clamps. Trim the bottom of the cup so that it won't show. Many doll-makers take pride in using only husks, so they remove the cup and stuff the doll with more husks. However, the cup gives added strength and protection to the delicate skirt, especially when stored away in a box.

Many people like cornhusk dolls with no features. Experiment. Leave a doll with a blank face. You can always add features later. Putting two dots for eyes and a line for the mouth is quite easy for anyone to do. Use marking pens, or showcard or watercolors.

Now your lady is ready to decorate your table, sideboard, or knickknack shelf. Make another one in a smaller size, and you will have a mother and daughter. Adult cornhusk dolls are usually 7" tall. The children measure 5". The wires for the arms should be only 5" long, and the skirts will be 2" shorter than those of the mother.

As soon as you have become proficient in making the all-in-one doll, try making the doll with the separate head.

4

The Separate-Head Doll with Ingrown Hair

Ingrown hair on a cornhusk doll looks so professional that most beginning doll-makers think that the procedure for making it is difficult to follow. They shy away from trying to insert the hair in the head first. It's very simple. Just follow the directions and the pictures. Substitute any other material you wish, if you don't care to use cornsilk. If you'd rather add hair later, disregard the instruc-

Insert cornsilk.

Wrap and pad head.

29

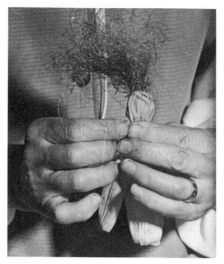 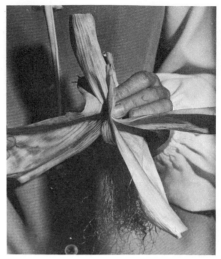

Squeeze at neck.   Arrange body husks around the head.

tions concerning the hair.

Everyone should try both ways of making cornhusk dolls, the all-in-one doll and the doll with the head separate. When making the separate-head doll, you can use shorter husks. You can also make taller dolls. When working with colored husks, you **must** make the head separately. Otherwise, the colored husk would be stretched across the face area. The neck of the all-in-one doll is small and pretty; but the neck of the separate-head doll is stronger.

Pick out two nice clean pieces of husk for the head. Insert the cornsilk, with the dark part uppermost, between the two pieces of husk. Tie tightly with a tying strip. This will be the top of the head.

Fold all the husk down until it measures about 1". Pad and wrap until the head size is reached. Flip down each piece of husk, smoothing over face area. Tie tightly at neck. Leave the hair sticking straight up until the doll is finished. This keeps the hair out of the way and protects it from getting broken.

Put the head to one side for a minute, while you arrange the rest of the husks. Take 7 pieces of husk as you did for the all-in-one doll. Two are for the dress, 1 for the apron, 2 for the sleeves, and 2 for the arms.

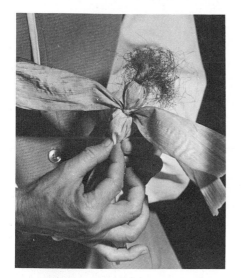 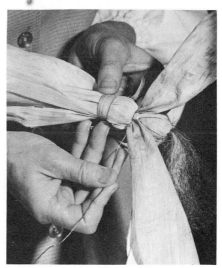

Squeeze at waist, then tie.   Insert wire.

Now, pick up the head and arrange the husks around it. With the head in the middle, place the apron and dress piece in front of the face and the other dress piece at the back of the head. Push sleeve and arm pieces in between these front and back pieces on each side. Grip firmly and tie.

Pull down hard on the base of the head to settle the neck firmly into the other pieces of the doll. Bring skirt front and apron down in front; bring skirt back down in back. Pad chest area with cloth, husk, tissue paper or any other filler material you prefer. Gather the husks at the waist and tie.

Measure and cut the wire for the arms as you did in chapter III. Push the wire through the neck. (This operation is more difficult with the separate-head doll, because of the increased density of the neck.)

Form arms as for the all-in-one doll and bend them down toward the apron.

Run a line of glue around the inside of the skirt so that the filling will stick permanently. Stuff the body with filler material, then insert the styrofoam cup.

Pin side seams of skirt. If the skirt isn't wide enough to go around

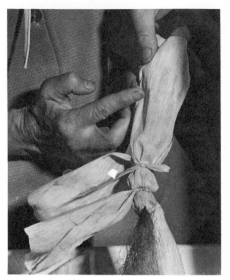

Pin the side seams.

Clip skirt to cup.

Trim the apron.

Trim hair.

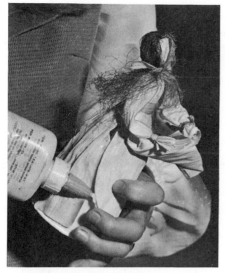 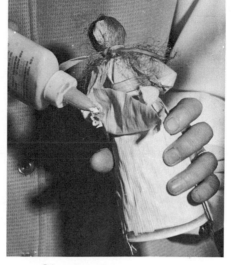

Glue seams.   Glue hands to apron.

the cup, insert a patching piece of husk into each side. (See chapter 6.)

Pin or clip the skirt to the cup until dry.

Trim the apron, bend the arms down, and pin the hands to the corners of the apron.

Dampen the cornsilk hair, handling it very carefully. It is so fragile that it will break if handled roughly. Tie it gently around the neck. Trim excess from around the face, using either straight or curved scissors, whichever is easier for you. Arrange the hair, making the style as simple or as elaborate as you wish.

Allow the doll to dry. Then, remove all pins and clamps, one at a time, gluing each seam as the pin is withdrawn. Clamp carefully and allow the glue to dry. If you want to strengthen your doll, take out the styrofoam cup, run several lines of glue around the outside of it, then put it back inside the skirt. Clamp all around. Trim the bottom of the skirt to match the length of the cup.

When the glue is dry, remove the clamps and your doll is done. If you would rather not make the hair ingrown, just omit it, and add curls later. Curls are explained in chapter 6.

Now that you have made lady dolls, make a man doll to go with them.

5

The All-in-One Man Doll

After cutting the base from the wet husks, arrange your pieces in this order: 2 sleeve pieces in the middle, then on each side an arm piece, a jacket piece, a leg piece. Remember that the largest husks will be for the legs, then next in order of size will be the jacket pieces, the sleeves and the arms.

Hold the 2 sleeves face to face; put the 2 arms on the outer sides. Place jacket pieces next to the arms, then add the legs to the outside of the jacket pieces. Gather and tie 2" from the end.

Roll this 2" length into a ball and pad it with husks or paper, wrapping around and around until the head is the size you want it to be. The man's head should be larger than the lady's.

(These instructions are for an all-in-one doll. If you prefer to make the man with the head separate, just follow the instructions for the head in chapter 4, then continue here with the rest of the doll.)

Flip all the pieces up over the head, one by one, smoothing the best one over the face area.

Measure a wire fingertip-to-fingertip length. (This will be about 8", since the arms of the man will be longer than those of the lady.) Cut the wire and insert it through the neck, keeping it under the arm and sleeve husks. Wrap and form the arms and sleeves exactly as

34

Husks spread out with tray.

Hold husk like this.

Insert leg wire.

you did those of the lady doll. For other styles of coats, you may prefer to have the sleeves straight. If so, pin the seams down the arms with no puffing.

Double the jacket and leg pieces over each other in front. Pad the chest cavity. Tie the waist strip in front instead of in back. Let the ends hang down in a sash effect, or clip them off close.

Cut 2 wires the length that you want your man's legs to be, 6" or 7" long. This measurement allows 1" extra for the length of the foot.

Insert these wires up into the body as far as the waist. Wrap rags or tissues around each wire. Shape leg husk around thigh of the doll. Pin the leg seam as far down as the knee. Gather husk at knee and, using a tying strip, wrap a puttee around the lower leg down to the ankle.

Tie it there with a strip or hold it with a pin or clamp. Cut off the husk 1" below the ankle. Bend it forward at a right angle to shape the foot, then clamp. Make the other leg just like the first. Be sure that the stuffing for each leg is the same thickness.

If you want your man to wear long pants, just pin the husks all down the inner seams of the legs.

Trim the lower edge of the jacket straight across.

For the drying process, you may find it easier to hang the man up, rather than to lay him down. (He probably won't be able to stand yet.) Tie a string around his waist and hang him to the clothesline or to a doorknob or chandelier. If air circulates around him, he'll dry quickly.

When your doll is dry, take out all pins, one at a time, and glue the seams, as you did for the lady doll.

For the man's hat, cut an oval from a damp piece of husk 2" long. Soak it for another half-minute. Hold it over a bottle cap of the screw-on type. Now, make a depression by pushing a marble down into the husk. The indentation made by the marble will just fit the head of your litttle man. When the husk dries, take out the marble, turn the husk upside down, and there you have a traditional pilgrim's hat!

Glue it to the man's head, pressing it firmly in place with your

Wrap the puttee.   Cut off at length of foot.

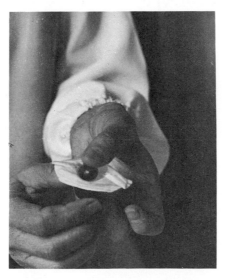

Marble pushed into a husk.

fingers until the glue sets. Never pin the husks when you're gluing. The glue will dry onto the point of the pin. Then, when you pull out the pin, the dried glue will tear a hole in the husk. When gluing, always hold the parts in place with clamps, rubber bands, ties, or your fingers.

It is sometimes difficult to make the man doll stand up. It's a good idea to glue the feet onto a platform made from a tiny board or piece of bark. First, cover the bottom of the feet with glue. Then clamp them securely to your platform.

Moisten the husks at the knee joints and bend the legs until he balances successfully on the platform. When the glue has dried, remove all clamps from the doll except those on the feet. Leave those until last. Then, carefully remove the clamps from the feet, and your man will stand.

Now that your man is finished, and you have a lady or two, arrange them carefully as a table centerpiece or decorative scene for the sideboard. You may need some accessories. Would your lady like a broom or a butter churn? How about a musket or a hatchet for the man? Instructions for these and others follow in the next chapter.

6

Accessories

Accessories for the arrangements give your dolls personalities. They range from butter churns, brooms, and rolling pins to baskets, hatchets and guns. The little people can be arranged to portray almost any scene and the cornhusks can be used to build everything needed in the way of "props," such as tables, boxes and benches. Rugs may be woven of husk or leaf strips, plain or dyed. Dying the husks gives the doll-maker a chance to create colorful dresses, aprons, overalls, hats and shoes. You may decorate with stripes, polka dots and other geometric designs on the skirts, bodices, and sleeves of the different items in the dolls' wardrobes. Some people like to use cotton materials, always using plain colors teamed with the tiniest of prints. Other doll-makers like to work with crepe paper. It's strictly a matter of choice.

THE THANKSGIVING TURKEY

Since the cornhusk dolls are used mostly for Thanksgiving decorations, you should learn to make a turkey to go with the pilgrim family. This step-by-step procedure is more complicated than that followed in making the dolls. Once you've made a turkey, though, you have learned the skills needed to make other animals and birds for your scenes and centerpieces.

Pick out 2 pieces of husk, 1 slightly larger than the other. Dip

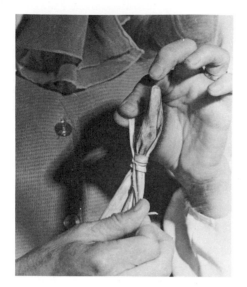 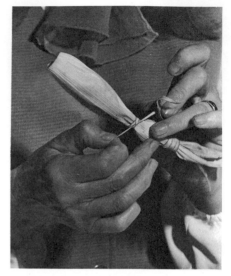

Turkey neck tie.   Turkey waist tie.

them in water, soak for about half a minute, shake off the drops of water, and lay the smaller one on top of the larger.

Gather the two husks together and hold tightly while you push a wad of stuffing into the space for the head. Use tissues, rags, or small pieces of husk for the stuffing. Tie a strip around the base of the head.

Start rolling this strip, winding it puttee-fashion to form the neck of the turkey. It will need about three complete turns. Tie at the lower end of the neck with a tying strip. Leave the pointed ends alone for now. They'll be trimmed later, becoming the beak and wattles.

Stuff the body cavity with more wadding, using a proportionately larger amount than you did for the head. The body should be at least 3 times as large as the head is. After stuffing, tie with a strip. Put the body aside while you make the legs.

Lay a piece of wire 3" long at the edge of a husk which is slightly longer. Roll the wire up in the husk. Tie about ½" from each end.

Now take up the body and spread the tail piece out and down as far as it will go. Put a drop of glue in the intersection of tail and

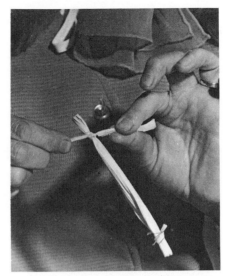

Roll the legs.   Tie ends of turkey legs.

body. Lay the piece of cornhusk-wound wire in this glue. Fold up
the tail feather against the body and pin it to hold securely.

Bend the legs and feet to the proper angles.

Squeeze the beak husks together and clamp. Stretch a rubber
band around the neck and body; leave on until dry. Trim the tail
with scallops for a feathery outline.

For wings, take a double thickness of husk and cut an oval, being
careful not to cut through the fold. Open it out to form a pair of
wings. Insert them between the body and the tail. Glue in place with
a drop of glue. The pin which is holding the tail up will hold the
wings in place until the glue dries.

Spread the feet wide and fill the cavities with glue. Clamp. Bend
the leg wires to balance the bird so that it will stand alone. This is
sometimes a little difficult; but if you keep bending and balancing,
you will find the right angle and your turkey will stand without
help. If you are unsuccessful, clamp the feet onto a piece of
cardboard or bark, and make your turkey stand in that way. Be
generous with the glue on the cardboard or bark. When it is dry,
remove clamps, rubber band, and pin. Trim the beak and wattles.

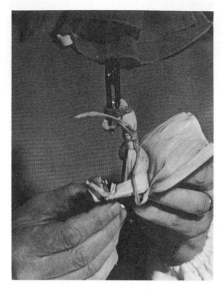

Insert leg piece into turkey and glue.

Clamp the beak.

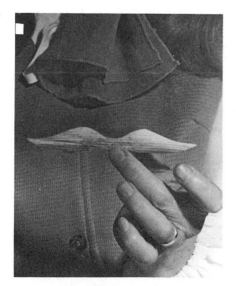

Wings.

Completed turkey.

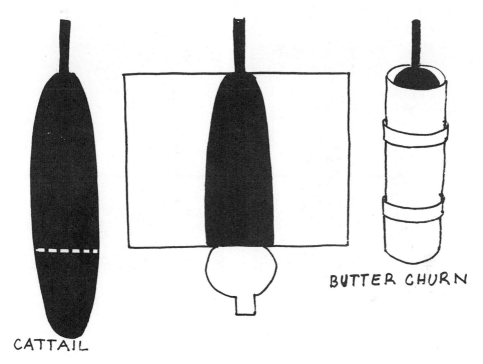

CATTAIL

BUTTER CHURN

BUTTER CHURN

Cut a 2" piece from a cattail spike, leaving about 5" of the stem attached. The stem will become the handle of the churn. Cut a piece of husk, following the pattern shown in the diagram. Put a drop of glue on the cut end of the cattail and press it onto the husk extension. Pull husk up and wrap it around the cattail. Wrap 2 tying strips around the churn, gluing the ends together. Clamp and allow to dry. Trim the 2 strips neatly.

BROOM

For the handle of the broom, use a wooden skewer, sucker stick, tree twig or cattail stem. Dip two 2" x 4" pieces of husk in water until pliable, then cut with scissors to make a fringe along the 2" sides. Put a drop of glue on the end of the husk and roll it around the broom handle. Apply another drop of glue and roll the other piece of fringe on top of the first one. When the fringe is completely wound, tie a strip around the top of it. Trim the bottom, and allow to dry.

Butter churn, broom, umbrella.   Making the broom.

UMBRELLA

Instructions for making the umbrella are very similar to those for the broom. Use the same material for the handle; stick, skewer, twig, or stem. Cut a rectangular piece of husk 2" x 4". Run a 2" line of glue onto the end of the handle and press the shorter edge of husk into the glue. Twirl the handle, wrapping the husk around it. Glue the other 2" edge flat. Tie a strip around end of umbrella. Pull top of husks out slightly.

MUSKET

The musket for the pilgrim is made from a goldenrod stem which has formed a ball around a grub. These deformed weed stalks are found along country roads and in fields. Cut the stalk right through the ball. Hollow out the cut surface, using the point of a knife. The other half of the ball can be attached to the other end of the gun. Scrape out its stem end so that the barrel of the gun will fit into it. Leave the cut end flat, to be used as a shoulder-rest.

If goldenrod stems aren't available, you may cut out a musket from either construction paper or thin cardboard.

Ax and musket.

Rolling pin, sprinkling can, and bucket.

AX OR HATCHET

The handle of the ax or hatchet is made from a sucker stick or wooden skewer 4" long for the ax or 2" long for the hatchet. Cut the blade from a piece of husk shaped like a bow tie. Cover with glue and fold in half over the end of the handle. Clamp until dry. The hatchet's blade should be smaller than that of the ax.

ROLLING PIN

Cut a stick 3" long for the handle. Cut several strips of wet husk about 1¾" wide. Cover the middle of the stick with glue. Wrap husk pieces around and around until the rolling pin has a diameter of ⅜". Glue the seam and tie in several places. Allow to dry. Then, cut off the ties.

SPRINKLING CAN

Cut a 1½" piece from a cattail spike. Cover with husk as you did the churn. Make a tiny hole with the point of a knife, and push in a 1" length of goldenrod stalk, the same kind as the one used for the musket. Push it into the piece of cattail on an angle, thus forming the spout. Make a handle from a strip of husk, gluing both ends to the body of the sprinkling can. Here, again, if you can't find weed

Milkweed-pod serving tray.   Lady's hat.

stalks, use a match stick, tiny roll of paper, or a narrow strip of cardboard for the spout. If you can't find cattails, make the body by forming a piece of husk into a tube. Glue and clamp until dry. Make a small hole in the husk with the point of a knife, insert the spout, and apply glue to the opening to hold the spout in place. Apply the handle as before.

SERVING TRAY

A milkweed pod makes a clever tray to hold flowers or fruit. Tiny straw flowers, rose hips, or silver shot make colorful additions to your doll settings. If you prefer to make a tray from husk, simply dampen a small piece the size you want and cut a rectangle from it. Pleat each corner and fold it up to look like the corner of a box. Clamp each corner. Allow to dry, then remove the clamps.

PATCHES

When pinning your seams, hold husk between thumb and forefinger, one on the inside and the other on the outside of the doll. In this way, you will be supporting the fragile husk during the pinning operation. However, no matter how careful you are, the husks will occasionally tear. All is not lost. Patches are easy to make and apply. Cut a piece of husk slightly larger than the hole. Glue all edges, and place patch under the torn piece. Clamp all around. When dry, remove clamps. When patched carefully, no one will know where the patch is. The husk blends in perfectly, becoming an almost invisible patch.

HATS

For the pilgrim lady doll, the traditional hat is explained in chapter 3. Notice that there are two ways to make it. You may pull the sides back first, then pull down the back part. Or you may pull the back part down first, and then pull back the sides. Try tying a strip around the neck of the doll, catching the material of the hat in it; tie in a bow in front, allowing the ends to hang loose, becoming the bonnet ties.

On little girls, allow the bonnet to hang straight down to the sides, with no ties. Fold the edges up along the bottom, if you like the Dutch style. The front corners may be folded up and back to frame the face. Shape while wet. Clamp all edges and corners until dry.

Other hats may be made by cutting the husks into squares, triangles, or circles. They are easier to handle if the husk is doubled. Glue 2 thicknesses of husk together and clamp along all 4 sides. After the basic hat is dry, it can be decorated with many things. It's

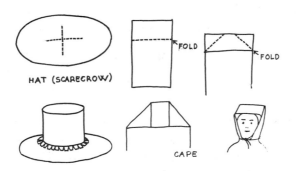

HAT (SCARECROW)

FOLD

FOLD

CAPE

sometimes easier to decorate the hats after they're attached to the dolls. Glue them to the tops of the heads and allow to dry. Then, cover each hat with glue and add bits of rickrack, lace or artificial flowers. Tiny gems or sequins add color and interest. Feathers add elegance. Loops of husk may be glued to the hatbrim, then laced with ribbons. You could tie any of these hats on with a narrow ribbon, instead of gluing to the head.

Try different styles on your dolls. A head covering for a peasant girl is made from a rectangle of husk. Pull down on both sides of the head. Pull the back 2 corners forward, crossing them under the chin. Pin these 2 corners on top of each other. Allow to dry. Remove the pin, then glue and clamp until dry.

Notice the headgear of the dolls in the Nativity scene. Cornhusk, when wet, is so easily formed into different shapes, that it's an ideal material for making clothing as well as boxes and bags. Drape the husks around the figures, tying them in place or clamping until dry. The tube-shaped hat is made from a rectangular piece of husk 3" long and 1" wide. Simply wrap the husk around the head, twisting it more tightly at the top to make it smaller there than at the bottom. Glue the seam and clamp until dry.

To make a hooded cape, take a 5" piece of husk and fold the short end down 1". Fold down the 2 corners, forming triangles. Glue and clamp until dry. Remove clamps, open the hood and glue to the head of the doll.

For a turban, wrap a strip of husk around the head until the desired size is reached. Tie the turban together in the front, allowing the ends of the tie to stick straight up. Trim them to a length of ½" and cut down into them several times to make a fringe.

A plain turban has no tie. Just glue the end of the strip in place, and clamp until dry. Remove the clamp, place on the doll's head, and glue into the position you want.

Instructions for the pilgrim's hat are in chapter 5.

Another man's hat is shown on the scarecrow in chapter 7. Different styles can be made by shortening or lengthening the height of the hat. For the brim, cut an oval 2" x 3". Cut a piece of husk 4" x 1". Slice ¼" slits in the long edge and fold them out. Glue the shorter ends together, making a tube. Now, glue the folded-over slits to the middle of the brim. Cut crosswise slits in the center of the brim, so that the hat will fit down over the doll's head. Allow to dry, then glue the hat to the head of the doll.

Still another style can be made by gluing a crown to the pilgrim's hat.

HAIR AND CURLS

Professional-looking hair is inserted into the top of the head before the husks are arranged. (See chapter 4.) Then, when the doll is turned right-side out, the hair will appear to be growing naturally. For your first dolls, you may prefer to make the hair separately as individual curls pushed up under the hat, or as a wig. Yarn, thread, excelsior, ravelled burlap, or cornsilk can all be made into hair for your dolls. If you wish to make a wig, stretch the material you choose across a piece of paper. Your hair material should be 2" deep. Run a line of stitching down the center, across all the threads of hair material. Run another line of stitching on top of the first. Then, carefully tear away the paper, and you have a flat piece of hair material with a center part. This can be either curled, braided, or left straight. Try it on the head of your doll and decide on the hairstyle you want to create. Then, cover the head of the doll

Curls.

with glue, place the hairpiece on it, and hold down carefully on all sides, using all your fingers pressing in from all angles. You may wind some string around the head, just tight enough to keep the hair in contact with the glued surface of the head. After the glue has dried, you can cut or curl or wave the hair any way you want.

To make curls from cornhusks, wrap wet husk strips around drinking straws. Clamp the ends of the husks with hair clips. Allow to dry thoroughly. When dry, remove the clips and slip the curls from the straws. Push ends of curls up under your doll's hat; arrange them to suit you. Run a line of glue up under the edge of the hat or bonnet and hold firmly for a minute until dry.

ANGEL

Make the doll as explained in chapters 2 or 4, with a few changes. Use one husk less, because you don't need the apron. Also, do not puff the sleeves. Allow them to hang loose, pinning each sleeve seam carefully. Make wings as you did for the turkey. Make different sizes, and fringe or scallop the edges. Glue them to the back of the doll. If you make more than one pair of wings, glue the larger pair next to the doll, then put the smaller pair of wings on top. Tie a

Angel and bird on tree.

Lapel doll with plain arms and kerchief.

Lapel doll with wired arms and hat.

ribbon to the waist of the doll with a long extension, so that it will be easy to hang the angel on the Christmas tree.

LAPEL DOLL

Fold a 6" or 8" piece of husk in half. This will make a doll 3" or 4" long. Gather and tie at the neck, 1" from the folded end. Twist a 4" piece of husk tightly to form a piece long enough for both arms. Insert it between the front and back husks, and tie the doll at the waist. Tie the end of each arm to hold the husk together. Spread the skirt wide. For a boy doll, split the skirt, and tie the two legs at each ankle. For larger dolls, you may like to braid some husks to form the arms. Or roll a wire in husk, as you did for the turkey's legs, and use it for the arms.

A tiny safety pin can be sewn to the back of the neck, so that you can pin the doll onto your coat or dress.

BASKETS

The Oval Basket

Dampen a piece of husk and fold it double. Cut an oval 2½" long and 1½" wide. Spread glue between the layers and clamp all

Baskets.

around. For the handle, cut a strip 3" x ½". Spread it with glue and fold over to measure ¼" wide. Clamp along the edge. Bend up the sides of the basket and clamp the ends of the handle to it, adding a drop of glue to each contact point. Allow to dry; then remove all clamps.

The Square Basket

For the body of the basket, you will need 7 narrow strips for the bottom and sides, 3 strips for weaving, and 1 narrow strip for the handle.

Wet the 7 strips and lay them on the table in front of you, four in a row. Weave the other 3 in the middle section, close together. Turn these 7 bottom pieces up to form the sides of the basket. Center a block of styrofoam in the middle, and pin the strips to it.

Wet the long strips. Weave the first one in and out, around the basket, tucking the end into the beginning of its row. Weave the other two in the same way, alternating the rows, so that the basket will be strong. Follow the diagrams while you work. As you weave, pin the strips to the styrofoam block.

Trim the 7 basic strips to within ¼" of the top row. Fold these original strips down around the top of the basket, alternating the fold to the inside for one strip and to the outside for the next. Clamp

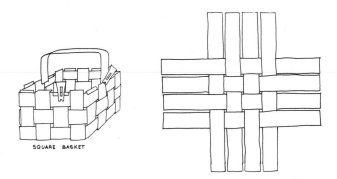

SQUARE BASKET

all around, one clamp holding 2 strips.

When dry, remove the clamps. Insert the ends of the handle and glue them to the inside of the basket. Clamp until dry.

BUCKET

Roll 1" strips around and around until you have a cylinder with a ¾" diameter. Glue seam at end of strip and tie until dry. Put several drops of glue into the middle to hold the inside spirals together. Cut a strip 3" x ⅛" for the handle. Put a drop of glue on each end of this strip, and push down into the sides of the bucket. No clamp is necessary to hold the handle. As the husks dry, the spirals on the inside of the bucket will hold the handle in place.

BIRD

Use one large section of cornhusk for the body and head. Gather the larger end with the inner part on the outside and tie. Turn right-side out. Stuff this tied end with soft paper to form the head. Pull the edges of the husk together until they meet. Tie at neck. Stuff the body, and glue the seam where the edges meet. Tie at beginning of the tail. Clamp the remaining husk for the tail and trim it evenly in a triangular shape.

For the wings, take 4 rectangular pieces of husk and glue them

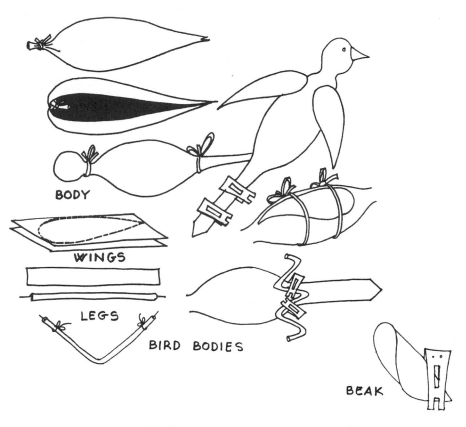

BODY

WINGS

LEGS

BIRD BODIES

BEAK

Wings.

Bird.

together in pairs. Cut into wing shapes. When the body of the bird is
dry, glue on the wings. If you want them to be folded close to the
body, tie them down until dry. If you prefer them to be outspread,
hold them until they dry.

For the beak, cut a piece of husk as shown in the diagram. Clamp
it together at the narrow end and spread out the oval end flat to dry.
Glue the oval end to the bird's head and hold it until dry.

To make the legs, roll 1 rectangular piece of husk on a wire. Run a
line of glue along the seam, and tie at both ends. Bend in half, then
back ½" from the middle. Follow the diagram, and bend the ends
forward to make the feet. Glue the center bent part to the bird, with
legs extended. Tie until dry.

ANIMALS

You will need 1 large section of cornhusk for the body and head;
1 rectangular piece rolled with the grain, a thin length of hemp rope,
or some cornsilk to form the tail; 4 rectangular pieces for the legs; 2
small pieces for the ears.

Gather the large piece (inside out) around the tail piece and tie.
Turn right-side out and fill with soft paper for the body of the

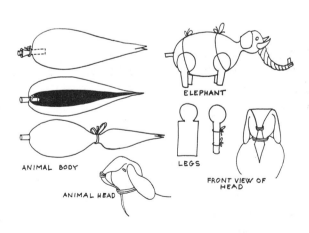

ELEPHANT

ANIMAL BODY

ANIMAL HEAD

LEGS

FRONT VIEW OF
HEAD

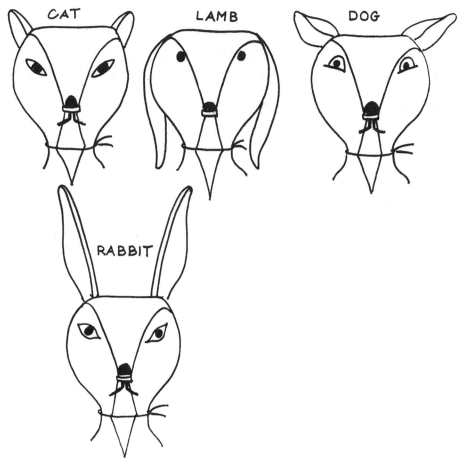

animal. Bring the edges together to meet. Tie at the neck.

For long-nosed animals such as elephants, stuff head, tie at end of head, then insert a length of wire as long as you want the trunk to be. Twist some husk around the wire and bend it to take the position the trunk is to be in. Cut the tip off square, tie it tightly, and allow to dry.

For short-nosed animals, fill the head, then flatten the front of the face. Fold this under twice and tie at the nose. Bend back to the neck and tie, tucking any remaining husk into the body seam. Study drawings carefully to see how this is done.

Cut legs according to the diagrams. Roll bottom part around wire, glue the length of the seam, and tie until dry. Dampen at joint,

Lamb.   Dog.

bend into the shape you want, and glue the upper flat part to the body of the animal. Tie gently but firmly until dry. The round disc-shaped parts which are glued to the sides of the animals blend in beautifully with the rest of the skin. They look like real muscles.

For ears, cut the shape according to the animal you are making. Fold each ear and clamp until dry. Remove the clamps and glue the ears to the animal's head. Hold them in place with your fingertips until the glue has set.

FLOWERS
General rules for making the basic flower

Use one complete husk for each flower. Dip it in water and cut off the husk 3" from the stem. Trim stem to about 1". Pull back each husk gently. These will be the petals for the flower.

Rose

Dip the basic flower structure in water. Round each husk piece with scissors. Curl back the rounded corners on tiny curlers made from 1" sections of drinking straws. Clamp each one and allow to dry. Leave a few inside husks in the center for a bud effect.

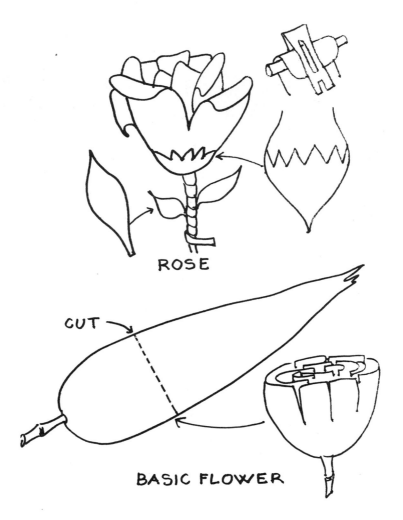

ROSE

CUT

BASIC FLOWER

For the calyx, use one large piece of wet husk to cut the sepals. Either follow the diagram, or accordion-pleat the husk and cut the end. Pleating the husk is the better way. When you open out your husk, you will have a whole row of sepals exactly the same. Dampen again and wrap this piece around the bottom of the rose. Tie with a tying strip. Twist the extra length of husk at the bottom of the sepals to make the inside of the stem.

Cut 1, 2, or 3 leaves, following the pattern. Wrap the stem with a strip of cornhusk, adding leaves as you go along. Glue and tie at the end.

Rose.

Chrysanthemum.

Chrysanthemum

Dip the basic flower in water. Tear the petals into strips down just to the stem. With scissors, round each end of the torn petals. Spread them apart. For the center of the flower, roll 2" fringed strips into a tight spiral. Remember to fringe and roll **with** the grain. Keep rolling your spiral until it is big enough to fill the center of the flower. Tie with a strip until dry. Fill this center area with glue and push into it the husk spiral. Hold it firmly with your fingers until the glue has set, just a few minutes. Cut and trim any bits that stick out. Make your sepal and stem piece as you did for the rose, and tie it to the stem of the flower. Cut some leaves, following the pattern. Wrap a strip of husk all the way down the stem, adding the leaves at intervals as you proceed. Anchor the winding strip at end of stem with a tie. A drop of glue at the stem end of each leaf and also at the bottom of the stem will strengthen the completed flower.

Peony

Dip the basic flower structure in water; then round the corners of the petals. Cut indentations in the upper edges of each petal. Bend back the petals. Add extra petals in the middle by cutting some from extra husks and gluing them to the center.

Peony and simple poppy.

Daisy.

Poppy.

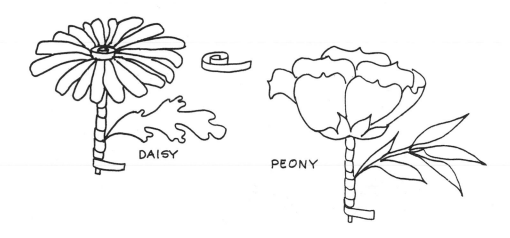

DAISY

PEONY

Make the standard sepal-stem piece and wrap and tie as you did before. Cut leaves, following the pattern. Wrap the stem with a strip, adding the leaves as you go. Glue and tie at the end. If you're not sure of the correct shape of a leaf or petal, look at a picture of the flower you want to duplicate. In this way, your flowers will look authentic and professional.

Daisy

Take your basic flower shape, dip in water, and pull the petals out so that they are perpendicular to the stem. Tear petals into 1" strips down to the calyx. Round the tips of the petals with scissors. Cut ½" strips and roll them into a spiral large enough to fill the center of the flower. Fill this empty center with glue and set the spiralled circle into it. Set the flower in a vase or water glass to hold it upright while the glue is setting. You may put a weight on the center to hold it firmly until the glue has set.

Make short sepals on the sepal-stem piece, wrap it around the base of the flower and tie. Make some leaves, following pictures for authenticity. Wrap a strip around the stem, inserting leaves at intervals, as before.

FRUIT DISH OR TRAY

Take 2 large pieces of damp cornhusk and glue them together. Trim to an oval shape. Press the wet husks around a jar, tie to the

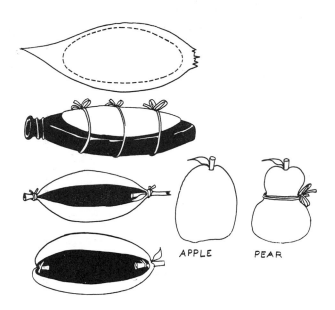

APPLE   PEAR

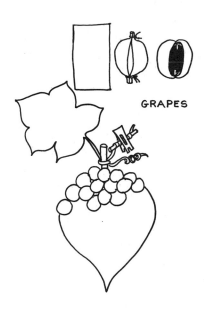

GRAPES

curved surface, as shown in the diagram, and allow to dry. Cut off ties.

PEAR

You will need 1 wide piece of cornhusk, and 2 small rectangular pieces for the stem and leaf of the pear. Roll one of the small pieces into a tube for the stem of the pear. From the other small rectangle, cut a leaf shape with an extra long stem, to facilitate the tying processes.

Tie the large husk at the growing end, inside out. Gather at the other end, inserting the leaf and stem into the second tie. The space in between these two ties is the height of the pear. Cut off excess husk.

Turn right-side out and fill with soft paper. Pull leaf away from stem a little, to make it look natural. Pull husk edges together at the seam. Tie a strip around the fruit 2/3 of the way up from the bottom, thus forming the shape of the pear. Remove the tie when the husk is dry, and glue the seam.

APPLE

You'll need 1 wide piece for the body of the apple and 2 small pieces for the stem and leaf. Roll 1 of the small pieces into a stem and cut the other piece into a leaf, as you did for the pear.

Tie the large husk at the growing end, with the inner side out. Gather and tie at the other end, after inserting the stem and leaf. The space between the 2 ties is the height of the apple. Cut off excess husk.

Turn right-side out; then fill with soft paper. Pull edges of husk together and pin the seam. Allow to dry. Remove pins and glue the seam.

GRAPES

You will need many small pieces of cornhusk. Dampen each one, then tie at each end with the inner part out. Turn right-side out and fill with soft paper. Bring seams together and allow them to dry.

To make a leaf, dampen a large husk and cut out a grape leaf from it.

For the base to hold the grapes, cut ½" from the stem-end of a piece of wet husk. Gather and tie with a long tying strip, catching the stem of the leaf into the tie. Roll the 2 ends of the tie on drinking straws and clamp. When the base, leaf, and tendrils are dry, remove the clamps and straws. Glue the grapes to the base, heaping them up near the top and tapering them near the bottom to form a realistic-looking bunch.

BANANA

For the banana you'll need 1 very long piece of cornhusk. Wet it and gather at both ends, tying securely. Fill with soft paper. Bring the edges together and either pin the seam or tie.

Run a string from one end to the other and pull to bend the fruit into an arch. Tie tightly. When the banana is dry, remove the string and glue the seam.

7

Decorating with Cornhusk Dolls

THANKSGIVING SCENE #1

Arrange your dolls in any grouping you wish. The one shown is traditional, using the family with the turkey. When the family is go-

Thanksgiving scene (1).

ing to church, the man leads and the woman follows. He always carries a musket. Trees may be made from dried weeds or the tassels from the corn. Anchor them in florists' clay, modeling clay, or a block of styrofoam. Cover the base of your choice with burlap or cornhusk.

THANKSGIVING SCENE #2

You may mix your cornhusk dolls with other decorative items if you are careful to keep them in proportion. Don't allow anything to overshadow the dolls. **They** are the center of interest and should not be crowded out of the scene, either by the size or color of other objects. The turkeys, cornucopia, and gourds shown are all of a very small size, so that the dolls are the focal point of the scene.

Thanksgiving scene (2).

Nativity scene.

NATIVITY SCENE

Make your cornhusk dolls by following the directions in chapters 3, 4, and 5 allowing the sleeves to hang straight down to the hands. Capes can be draped over the shoulders of the wise men, using different colored husks. The turban is made by rolling a piece of husk tightly around the head of the doll. Glue the ends down. The turban may be left plain; decorated with gems; or tied with a tying strip, then feathered by slitting the ends of the tie.

The hair and beards are all made from cornsilk. Other hair materials may be used, if you prefer.

Instructions for making the lamb are found in chapter 6.

The bench is a cardboard box covered with burlap. Cornhusks may be used to construct all sorts of tables, chairs, boxes, or platforms. Simply cover cardboard boxes or pieces of styrofoam with wet cornhusk, pinning in place until dry. Then, remove the pins and

Scarecrow.

glue at the seams. Clamp or tie the husks in place until the glue dries.

HALLOWEEN SCARECROW SCENE

Make a large cornhusk doll, splitting the skirt pieces to make two legs. Allow the arms to stick straight out from the body. Color the face orange like a pumpkin, or leave it the natural husk color. Add features, as shown in the picture, using a magic marker.

For the base, cut a block of styrofoam 4" square and 1" thick. Styrofoam blocks may be purchased in department stores, dime stores, or hobby shops. Cut a 16" strip of bamboo curtaining to cover the sides of the styrofoam block. Other fence-type materials could be used, such as bark or twigs, attached by tiny tacks, thumb tacks, or long pins. If none of these materials is available, a brown velvet ribbon will do, attached with pins. Glue the end of the ribbon neatly flat. Another, simpler way to make the fence, is to fit the styrofoam block into a cardboard box and then paint the fence on the sides of the box.

For the costume of the scarecrow, cut a piece of burlap or scrap material into a rectangle measuring 3" x 6". Fold in half crosswise; cut a semicircle in the middle. This becomes the head opening when the burlap is opened flat. Make a slit down the back so the garment will fit over the head. Dress the doll. Pin or glue the edges of the slit together. Tie the garment at the waist with a piece of burlap or string.

Insert an 8" dowel up into the doll. Push the other end into the styrofoam.

Push small pieces of dried weeds or artificial flowers and greenery into the styrofoam to make the field or garden which your scarecrow is guarding.

CRUCIFIXION PLAQUE

Cover a piece of masonite or heavy cardboard with burlap or velvet. Fit into a frame. Put together a cross of twigs or pieces of rolled cornhusk. Make a man doll, using only 4 husks, following the instructions in chapter 4 or 5. Tie the legs at knees and ankles. Tie the arms at elbows and wrists. Drape the body with husk pieces as shown in the picture. Arrange the figure on the cross and tie and tack it as shown. Then, mount it on the backing, using either glue or tacks. Snip off the ties when the husks are dry.

Crucifixion plaque.

Fungus plaque.

FUNGUS PLAQUE

The background in the pictured plaque is a piece of driftwood. Any sturdy backing can be used, but a weathered board gives your wall decoration a rustic character. The fungus shown was found on a fallen tree. After smoothing with a file, you'll be able to fit it snugly against the backing. Put a screw through the board and into the fungus, holding the two firmly together. Then, decorate the board with dried weeds such as ragweed, cattails, and milkweed pods, some closed and some open with the silk and seeds showing. After all the decorative weeds are glued in place, spray the whole thing with hairspray. Glue the doll to the shelf formed by the fungus.

FRUIT AND FLOWER ARRANGEMENTS

The dish of fruit is a striking sight when set against the natural wood of a walnut chest or any other dark background. The flowers can be grouped in a vase or basket in any pleasing arrangement. Here, you must follow your own instincts. Cornhusk is such a versatile material that it can be re-wet and shaped if the form doesn't quite come up to your expectations the first time.

Try adding cornhusk flowers to natural flower bouquets and

planters. Protect the stems from getting wet. Either wrap with waterproof material or insert stems in glass tubes. The contrast between the ivory of the husk and the colors of the flowers and plants helps make a very attractive centerpiece.

TRIMMING CHRISTMAS TREES

Cornhusk dolls, birds, animals and fruit make handsome decorations, showing up well against the evergreen boughs. The Garden Center of Greater Cleveland had an unusual and beautiful display of trees decorated by their member Garden Clubs for a recent holiday exhibit. The ladies of the club made cornhusk dolls, knitted tiny booties and mittens, and baked the cookies. These were to personify the gifts which are given year-round, not just at Christmastime. The dolls of cornhusk stole the show.

Another attractive entry was named the Northwest Tree. It was decorated with cornhusk dolls, red bells and balls made of yarn, and strings of popcorn. Here, again, the soft ivory color of the dolls showed off to perfection against the dark green background.

Try using your cornhusk-doll art in different ways. You'll be surprised and happy to find out how many places the products of your handiwork brighten and beautify your home.

Beverly and clown.

8

A Money-Making Project

Selling cornhusk dolls can become a good source of revenue for either one person or a group of people. Whether the money is for charity or for personal profit, if you're interested in selling the dolls, plan carefully with a business-like attitude toward the law of supply and demand. Approach the owners of gift shops, arts and crafts galleries, beauty parlors, and flower shops. They often will take a dozen dolls on consignment. Commissions vary from 10 per cent to 30 per cent.

Your local library, bank, or church might welcome a display of the dolls. (This is free publicity; and an identifying sign with your display may bring in orders.) Make sure that you always show well-made, handsome dolls. Never allow a poorly-made doll to be seen. Dismantle it immediately and make it over.

A cooperative can be formed by a group of doll-makers, such as a garden club. Some of the members can specialize in making certain parts. For example, an expert on hats will make nothing but hats. Another member who is exceptionally good at making baskets will concentrate on them. This system produces a large quantity of merchandise. Other members of the club who don't make dolls could handle the book-keeping and selling.

KITS OF MATERIALS

Getting materials for the dolls is often a chore, especially in areas out of the corn belt. Modern Americans are usually in a hurry. Many of them would prefer **not** to gather, dry, sort, and store the husks. They'd rather buy the material, and they're willing to pay a good price for them.

Packaging the materials needed for making the dolls is time-consuming, but quite simple. Here are the details on how to make up the kits, using the lady doll kit as an example.

First, arrange three cartons in a row on the far side of your work table. Label each one according to the part which it will hold. Now, separate your husks into the different size pieces needed. Wet and tie together those that are used together. For instance, take 2 sleeve pieces and 2 arm pieces and tie them together with a tying strip. Put a blue dot on it. Do the same for the dress and apron pieces, identifying the package with a red dot. Another package of tying strips and husks for accessories will have an orange dot on its tie. (Beginners are often confused by the different size husks needed. It's very helpful to have them packaged this way.) As you sort the husks, put in a separate pile the cleanest and widest ones, to be used for the heads. After you've tied all the packs, spread them out to dry.

When all are dry, toss each one into its respective carton. In the first one, you'll have the packs of dress pieces. In the second, the packs of arm and sleeve pieces. In the third, you'll have the packs of accessory pieces.

Now, arrange piles of wires, paper napkins, cornsilk, and paper bags. Add a stack of styrofoam cups and a stapler. Fill each lunch bag with a head husk, a package from each of the cartons, a cup, wire, napkin and a small bunch of cornsilk. Each bag holds everything needed to make a doll except glue and pins.

Last, staple the bag shut and mark on it the name of the doll to be made, with a list of its contents and the color keys.

Follow this same procedure for kits to make other dolls.

WHERE TO SELL THE DOLLS AND KITS

Bazaars, art shows, doll fairs, historical society shows, and club meetings are all good places to show and market your dolls. You'll find that the kits of materials will sell quickly to the hobbyists. You may make more money on the kits than you do on the dolls!

PACKAGING

Wherever you go to sell your dolls, take along a supply of plastic bags with wire closures. A doll in a transparent bag advertises itself. Often, someone will buy only one doll, then want another one later. An identifying card attached to the doll will give your name and address so he can order more.

Other people prefer to order, pay by check, and have the art work sent to them by mail. People expect to pay for postage and shipping, so charge for this service.

When mailing, pack each doll in a box. Allow plenty of room to stuff crumpled tissue paper around your dolls so they'll arrive in perfect condition. Shoe boxes make good shipping containers until your business bets big enough for you to afford a personalized package.

PRICES

At the bazaars and shows, take along as many dolls as possible to display and sell. Arrangements such as the crucifixion plaque, Thanksgiving and Nativity scenes, and the doll on the fungus shelf command higher prices than the single figures.

Are other cornhusk dolls for sale in your area? It's wise to keep your prices as close as possible to those of the competing dolls. Rules on pricing are extremely difficult to make. A doll which will sell for $6.00 in a gift shop will often sell for $3.00 at a bazaar. Your locality determines the prices you ask. Remember, you always

bring down a price easily, but you can rarely raise one without em-
barrassing questions being asked.

The law of supply and demand should always govern your
business. Cornhusk dolls are in style year-round, but make sure you
have a supply ready for the holidays. Crucifixion plaques sell well at
Easter, so make them in January. Work on Thanksgiving turkeys
and Christmas tree angels from September on. Give yourself plenty
of time so you won't be rushed. Your doll-making will remain an
enjoyable pastime as well as a money-making project.

DEFINITIONS

CALYX	Outer series of floral leaves
CORN BELT	Iowa, Illinois, Minnesota, Indiana, Nebraska, Ohio, Missouri, South Dakota, Kansas. (In Canada, corn grows in Ontario, Manitoba, Quebec)
CORNCOB	The center of the ear
CORNHUSK	A special kind of leaf which encloses and protects the ear
CORN LEAF	A leaf growing at the joint of the stem, or cornstalk
CORNSILK	Threads that run up the rows of kernels and stick out of the husks at the top of the ear
CORN TASSEL	Growth at top of the cornstalk, containing hundreds of flowers
FUNGI	A group of simple plants that have no green coloring matter, stems, leaves, or flowers. (Pictured in this book is a shelf fungus that grew on a tree.)
GOUACHE	A method of painting with opaque colors that have been ground in water and mingled with a preparation of gum
GRUB	Any soft, thick insect larva
MILDEW	A superficial growth, usually thin and whitish, produced often by dampness
PUTTEE	A strip wound spirally around the lower leg
RAFFIA	A fiber used for tying, basketry, and hat-making
ROSE HIP	The ripened false fruit of a rose bush
SEPAL	A leaf or division of the calyx
SILAGE	Fodder converted into winter feed for livestock
WATTLE	A fleshy piece of skin hanging from the chin or throat